Inner GYM

Trick of Parenting your Mind and Body to Live a Life of Happiness, Fulfillment & Overwhelming SUCCESS

Rajashree Chakraborty
Happiness Life Coach

About the Book:

Inner GYM is a book that trains you to be an Evolved & Healthy Version of YOU through Simple yet Effective Techniques in just 21 days. It helps you acquire Useful Habits through daily GYM sessions using Situational support strategies.

This book is a prescription to all of you out there looking for Health, Happiness and Success. There are so many books available today which provide you a whole lot of information on this topic. But what we see is that even if you gain adequate knowledge from reading the books, but most of the time, they are complicated and challenging to implement. Knowledge without action brings no result and takes us nowhere. So, we still continue our search for ways of staying healthy & happy and move on to the next book. The Habits mentioned in Inner GYM are simple, effective, and used for thousands of years. Even a 10-year-old can easily follow the recommended actionable. This book gives you techniques of what you should do, guides you on how you should do them, and how you can overcome any obstacles in your way in putting your knowledge into practice. It enables you to develop strategies on how you can form your new habits and align your Body-Soul-Spirit to exist in a harmonious way.

This book includes many research work-based information from worldwide, which sets the base for you to understand the concepts better & make your reading more insightful. It also has many wisdom quotes of famous and wise people and many real-life scenarios that will make your reading journey more exciting, and enable you to relate to the concepts better.

After reading this book you will get the following benefits–

1. You will experience Self-awareness

2. Realization of life purpose

3. Have Raised consciousness

4. You will learn how simple daily rituals can boost your health and well-being.

5. Your stress, anxiety goes down.

6. You learn how to derive Happiness from your work and, as a result, get recognition, appreciation, and even promotion in your workplace.

7. Your relationship with others improves.

8. You learn to control your mind and develop better focus.

9. You learn the technique of keeping your mind young by learning constantly.

10. You move ahead in your life from a different perspective.

11. You learn the trick of having total control on your will power and emotion.

12.   You learn the trick to keep your body and mind in total alignment.

I am confident that this book will make a difference in your life because I have experienced immense benefit after using these techniques. I have also witnessed these prescribed GYM activities bringing fantastic results when implemented by others from different age groups and different walks of life. So, you can entirely rely on these tested tools of training your mind body spirit. Train your spirit to be a responsible guardian and become successful in your personal and professional life.

So, what are you waiting for? Learn the Trick of Parenting your Mind and Body and Live a Life of Happiness, Fulfilment & Overwhelming Success. Enjoy God's greatest gift to You- "Your Life." Grab your copy of INNER GYM now.

****

Table of Contents

1. Who Am I?

We are not human beings having a spiritual experience. We are spiritual beings having a human experience- Pierre Teilhard de Chardin[1]

****

This is the most vital question in our life.

Most of us live an entire life without delving deep into this concept of "Who I Am"? The answer to this question is the basic essence of our life and existence. This very idea has the answers and solutions to all the problems that we encounter in our life. The knowledge and understanding of this concept require an ocean of explanation. I will not be taking this up here in depth in this book. You will find a lot of

---

[1]https://www.brainyquote.com/quotes/pierre_t eilhard_de_chardi_160888

information in several web pages, spiritual, sacred or holy books. However, to give you a basic understanding on how we usually deal with this concept let us begin with a very common situation from our regular life. All of us have experienced a situation where we have received gifts either directly by ourselves or passively witnessed a family member or friend receiving a gift. Let us for a moment create a similar situation now. Suppose we have received a gift box from someone we love and with whom we want to spend the rest of our life. You get a beautiful box covered with beautiful colored paper, covered with a beautiful curly shiny ribbon and on top of it is attached an attractive card with the best wishes and love message on it. Now you are curious to know what is there inside the box. So, you read the red card with a smile and then very carefully open the orange ribbon, you unwrap the golden yellow gift-wrapping paper which is so carefully and skillfully concealing the surprise element inside it. You get a small green cardboard box; inside the box you get a beautiful blue designer pouch. You open the pouch and get a small violet velvet jewelry box. Finally, you open the violet box. As you uncover the wraps and labels one by one and move towards the original gift step by step, your feelings keep changing and moves from happiness to joyfulness to blissfulness to an ecstatic state of mind where you burst out with joy on finding out a sparkling solitaire popping out its head wanting to embrace your finger with a promise of an eternal commitment. Here, I am not trying to indicate by any means that happiness comes with such material possessions. In fact, on the contrary, I have written the first part of this GYM series on Happiness GYM, where I have covered in depth the strategies and GYM to embrace Happiness in your Life, and by no means is that eternal happiness dependent on material possessions. But the point to prove here is just that, for most of you such situations have occurred in your life. We need not focus on the solitaire here but the point is that we often spend some amount of time in uncovering and getting to know what the true gift is. Now can you draw any sort of connection with this example with our life? When you are asked to give your self-introduction what do you say socially? Check out if you too follow this pattern. We start with our name, and then say may be father's name, locality or country, educational qualifications and professional tags and labels. Pause and think for a while. In the social platform these labels and tags are actually being used to wrap our true self within. As we move ahead in our life the number of labels and tags increases and so does our EGO thus making it even more difficult to reach out to our true inner self. The shining diamond that we are gets more distanced by these acquired tags. Right from the moment we are born we get the first tag with name of our parents followed by our own name and place of birth. This gives us our first acquired certificate once "I am Born", The Birth Certificate. Remember, these tags do not define or reveal the true meaning of the "I" that we are seeking to find out. As life moves ahead and we keep on acquiring more and more certificates and designations, we finally find ourselves completely distanced and detached from our true identity and get layers of EGO encapsulating our true self. We get completely deviated from the original purpose of our existence. I hope this clears the point that I am trying to get to.

For the sake of brevity, I will restrain myself to just that when we are talking of "I" here, I is the Spiritual energy that is the actual me.

The soul (mind) or body are the worldly tools that I have and use to communicate and live in this life in the world. We say that the body belongs to me and hence refer to as "my body". Similarly, we say "my mind" just like we refer to any other material objects from my possession as my house, my book, my car etc. Even when we talk of relationships, we say my friend, my father, my son etc. So, our mind & body are our possessions that we get as our tool to communicate in this world and are our most precious possessions.

The Human being is believed to be composed of

- Spirit (I - the subject)
- Soul (My)
  - Mind
    - Conscious mind
    - Subconscious mind
  - Will
  - Emotion
- Body (My)

The Body serves the soul, the soul serves the spirit, the spirit serves the God. A balance and alignment of all the three is the key to a perfect life of well-being, fulfilment & happiness.

Let us start our journey of reading and understanding the content of this book with a story of a family situation. Such situations happen in our life quite often, in our family or amongst friends or even in our offices. Can you imagine what happens if each member in a family thinks in different ways? Say your mother asks what food you would like to have today? You say you would like to have chicken; your brother says he won't eat chicken but will have mutton. Your sister who is very conscious of how attractive she would like herself to look, says, "No, I am neither going to eat chicken, nor mutton. I will simply have some vegetables". What happens to your mother? Can you imagine what she is going through? Either she has to cook different dishes to satisfy all of you or she will either satisfy one and let the others get unhappy. A very tricky but common problem in many households today where people from two or three generations are living together. This happens because of the fact that the dietary requirements change with age. Older age group people will have preference for low salt, no sugar diet and younger ones will prefer sweet rich diet. There can be hundreds of choices, preferences and prescriptions which can be the determinants for menu selection in the modern households. If you face a similar situation, what will be your plan of action? This was just a very simple example which is very common in most families. The problem is not only for those who cannot offer all the dishes because of financial issues but also for people who cannot cook so many dishes due to shortage of time issues. However, the good news in this case is that we still have a probable solution and can cook to each one's likings. Now imagine the same family is planning a vacation and you say you would love to go for a hill site, your brother says he would prefer the seas and your sister chooses a historical site with monuments and forts and deserts. What will your parents do? In the food scenario there was still a chance to cook for all three of you. Here chances are higher that at least two of you are bound to be unhappy. These types of clashes are quite common in our families and there are quite a number of occasions when we compromise with our likings and settle down to accept others choices. Every time we do something against our will, we are actually causing a point of stress to occur in us. Every time we experience such a situation where there is a differcncc in opinion or a clash of ideas, we become unhappy.

If we now focus our attention to our own self, you will realize a similar situation is going on inside us day in and day out. Yes, I'll explain. Our Physical body, Our Conscious Mind, Subconscious Mind, Our Will, Our Emotions and Our Spirit are all members of a family. Each member is not only connected but also very closely dependent on each other. As a result, whenever there is disagreement between each other we experience a stimulus that affects us in a way which in turn affects our health. This is the reason, when I spoke about Happiness in my Previous Book "Happiness GYM- How to Become Successful in Career & Relationships & Live Happily Ever After" Happiness was defined as "Happiness is when we are in a balanced state of mind that is caused by the perfect harmony of

- Physical
- Mental
- Emotional
- Intellectual
- Spiritual
- Social
- Educational/ Occupational
- Financial
- Environmental well-being."

Each such internal clash disturbs us in ways which are manifested through our illness of body or stress and illness in mind. We are simply not at peace. Everywhere around the world we can see there is so much of issues with physical, mental, emotional health. In spite of staying in the world where we are having abundance all around us, why are we not Happy? Technological advancement has been phenomenal and has given us every comfort in life that we could ask for. Why then are we not satisfied?

External clashes are still acceptable and outside our sphere of influence. We cannot ask our brother to not have mutton and sister to not have vegetables and tell her to choose chicken because I am preferring. Whether or not they agree with you is not in your control and completely their prerogative. What is shocking is that we have gradually lost control on ourselves. There are times when our body wants chicken but mind instructs us not to eat chicken and adopt the vegan lifestyle. Have you ever experienced such situation? Maybe not chicken but coffee, alcohol or cigarette? I am sure by now most of you could identify experiencing such a scene in your life and nod in agreement with a smile of guilt on your face, saying "yes, it happens quite often".

We have been staying with these internal clashes for all these years now and in fact fail to even identify and realize what damage we have been doing to ourselves in the long run.

In this book I am going to discuss more aspects of what actions we can take up so that our body, mind and spirit acts in total agreement & alignment. We need to parent and guide our babies so that we can live a life of fulfilment and Happiness. A specially Designed GYM with Diet will make your journey enjoyable and full of realizations and adaptations.

****

"So many people spend their health gaining wealth, and then have to spend their wealth to regain their health." — A. J. Reb Materi[2] ("Health Quotes | Inspiring Thru Quotes")

****

---

[2] https://www.yourselfquotes.com/health-quotes-for-body-mind-soul/

2. Body- Mind Interactions

"Health is like money; we never have a true idea of its value until we lose it." – [3]Josh Billings (MindZip)

****

Human Body is the most complex machine that we have so far experienced and our knowledge is still limited on this subject. The Human body is divided into two distinct parts the physical or material part consisting of our body and the non-physical or immaterial part that consists of spirit, soul, mind, emotions. There are doctors who do the trouble shooting of our physical body and there are psychologists who take care of our mental and emotional aspects. Apart from these there are also evidences and accounts of several

---

[3] https://mindzip.net/fl/@edy1/quotes/health-is-like-money-we-never-have-a-true-idea-of-its-value-until-we-lose-it-57c3bf77-bb29-45d0-a4bb-17180e6840dd

symptoms and issues which can neither be explained by a doctor nor by a psychologist. There are new technologies and branches of healing coming up today to address such problems. Delving deep into the subconscious mind has also sometimes given answer to so many complaints. Past life regression therapy, Pranic healing, Chakra healing are examples of several branches which are gaining popularity to treat imbalance and improve wellness. The manifestation and experience of a problem happens as a result of several clashes within ourselves. We fail to recognize and give importance to our wishes and desires arising deep within. There are people who usually listen to their conscious mind, there are people who listen to their subconscious mind. There are so many imbalances that arises because of this conflict between our conscious and subconscious mind only. If we learn the why and how of this, we will be sorted and will be able to deal with our selves better. Though it is a complex subject but when understood it is simple to handle. The practice of the serics of GYM is the key to your Happiness.

If we talk about our body parts, we interact with the outside environment with our 5 senses. Apart from that our body hardware is made up of the organs, complex tissues, nerves, bones and blood.

A very large part about 90% of our mind is the subconscious part and our conscious mind is only 10% of the whole. Similarly, we have our Will Power which acts and uses energy to implement certain decisions taken by our mind and supervises that our body is executing the orders of the mind. Our emotions on the other hand are manifested through our body. When we are angry, we say that our blood is boiling, when we are scared or shocked, we say we are having goosebumps or we say that we have a hair-raising experience. When we are sad, tears roll down. Each one of us have experienced such instances in our life.

Before going further let us address one very important topic. This is a subject of interest for many of us. The topic is when we are saying – "My Body" who is this Me or who is the I. We say my house, my car, my pen, my phone, my father, my friend, my hand …… So, they are mine, I own them as my property or claim them as my close relation or acquaintance. As we say "My Body", definitely it means that that the body is not me. I am owning the body made up of physical matter. This is just my possession on earth through which I communicate to the world. Our body acts as the interface between our mind and the outside world on earth. If we talk about our Mind, Emotion and Will we see that there also we say- "My mind", My will power", "My emotions" so we can see that all these components of our soul are also acquired by us for existing on this earth. So, this Great Body-Mind Combination is our earthly possession acquired by us at birth and we are owners of this till we leave this world. The Subconscious mind is the only component that will be taken back by the I – "The Spirit". I am a pure form of divine energy; the Spiritual energy and I communicate with the world through the soul and body. The Subconscious mind records all our knowledge and experiences and keeps it stored like a hard disc. That is exactly the reason and basis of the modern healing techniques using past life regression. So next time just keep in mind that the wealth we accumulate in our lifetime in terms of money accounts only as our worldly possession and does not go beyond this life. The wealth that we acquire in terms of our Knowledge and experience are our true priceless possessions and accounts for our actual savings that we carry forward with us.

Let us now understand how the internal conflict affect our well-being. Hence forth whenever we encounter a difference of opinion or an internal disagreement, we will refer to it as a "CLASH". Each clash is a stimulus that causes disturbance and is a source of stress. Numerous such stimuli cause a disorder or disease in us.

What happens internally?
Suppose you like to smoke. All of us including you are aware that the cartons have a clearly written warning on them "Cigarette smoking is injurious for your Health." You read it but you can't resist. Your parents, husband or wife, friends all recommend you to stop smoking. But you are addicted. There are moments when you wish to quit smoking but you are not able to. Whenever you pass by your local cigarette store, you glance and go for it. There is a turmoil within you. Mind is saying "you should not", body is saying "One last time". Who is winning and who is losing in such a battle? Any idea? Apparently if you choose to smoke your body wins and your conscious mind loses, but, the internal disagreement that happened causes irreparable damage to your body which is more than what a cigarette does to you. Yes, you got it right. I repeat. "The damage caused due to

internal conflict is MUCH MORE than the damage that would be caused by smoking alone". I have seen thousands of people who have been chain smokers for years and have been quite fit and healthy. On the other end, I have also witnessed people developing cancers within 3 to 4 years of smoking. I am not advocating smoking through this writing, but what I am trying to say is that don't smoke with a guilt in your mind. That guilt and conflict within your mind and body causes you more damage than your cigarette.

The fight that we spoke about is not between your body and mind as it appears. It is actually a case in court by the two parties- your conscious and subconscious mind. Our conscious mind reads, listens and analyzes all the warnings and develops an opinion of what to do and what not to do. Subconscious minds record our experiences and stores it in our memory. Every time we smoke if we feel good then subconscious mind records and stores that feel good experience. Now if our Will Power is strong enough then it will direct our body to act as per "what our conscious mind says we should do" and stop us from smoking. This is the reason why we see if a person has strong will power then generally, he is capable of taking decisions and actions as per conscious analytical mind and very often they are more successful as compared to a weak-willed person. If we are able to quit smoking on one instance and then the next and so on gradually, we form a habit. If we are able to build up our habit then later on, we will not require the support of our will to put that extra effort to control our action. We will have achieved a behavioral change to this new habit of not smoking and our present experience gradually forms the recording in our subconscious mind and becomes integrated into our soul.

The example that I just now gave of a cigarette is just one instance. This happens with all addictions and all situations wherever we are supposed to take decision. Say for example when we choose what to wear in the morning before going to work, we more than often experience a "CLASH". When we choose our diet for the day we experience "CLASH". In fact, even before getting out of bed in the morning right from the time the alarm rings and our mind says to get out of bed and body feels to put off the alarm and stay in bed for a little while more, every moment we experience "CLASH". Every time we experience a "CLASH" and we choose to act against our bodily comfort or bodily desires we need our Will Power to intervene and use up extra energy from its store of energy. By the end of the day our will power battery charge gets drained and we feel heavy, tired and irritated. What can we do so that we do not have to use our will so often and stay fresh whole day along with full energy? We need to decide what we want to do and prepare a routine and adhere to it in such a way that it becomes our Habit. We need to prepare the routine in such a way that we incorporate feel good factors into it. The first day you have to get up say at 5:30 am you will need will power, second day you will need lesser will power, third day even lesser and gradually by the time you arrive on the 21st day, you will already have developed a habit of getting up at 5:30 and you will wake up automatically, without using your will power and without even your external alarm. You just have to take care that after waking up you engage yourself in some activity which gives you a great feeling that you love to enjoy- like an early morning walk or yoga or a simple meditation.

Obesity is a very big problem today. I have seen several obese people quite happy about it and not trying any means to control their diet. Its ok. There are problems with overweight. Who is denying the fact? But at least don't eat with guilt. That creates your food turn toxic to your body and you feel the adverse effects even before your obesity creates problem for you. Internal "CLASH" when mind says "don't eat" and body craves for more, causes more problem than obesity itself. Plan your diet in such a way that takes care of your conscious mind as well as satisfies your feel-good desires as recorded by your subconscious mind. Please do not eat with a mind full of Guilt.

****

3. Body-Mind Diet:

"Every time you eat or drink, you are either feeding disease or fighting it." — Heather Morgan[4]

****

Let us talk about what should be the diet for our Body & Mind.

I believe you are fully aware, at least your conscious mind is completely aware of what should be your proper diet for your body and physical health. Though it may vary depending on your gender, nature of work or lifestyle or any specific ailments that you may be having, with the exception of any person having any specific illness definitely, we propose a balanced diet with carbohydrates, proteins, vitamins, minerals and fat in recommended proportion. There are several diet patterns whereby you may choose to go for a vegan diet or you may include non veg depending on

---

[4] https://www.healthyharford.org/beware-diet-is-a-four-letter-word-2

your pattern of diet that you have been following for years. Just don't try to change anything drastically. What you can vouch for is local food which you can consume fresh, be it vegetables, fruits, milk, egg or fish or meat. Choose anything that has not reached you via numerous factory processing having a lot of harmful chemicals and preservatives added to it. Also, it is highly recommended to avoid meat and fish. Highly recommended are vegetables and fruits which are having grown through organic farming if it is feasible for you. Also, in today's scenario when we are completely racing with time, we often go for ready to eat packaged food which should be avoided by all means. Not only should we focus on the local variety of fruits, vegetables and fishes but also we need to take care that we eat our food within 3 hours of being cooked. Freshly cooked homemade locally available food is the best choice for our health and immunity. In situations where you are running short of time go for quick meals with boiled vegetables or salads with fresh vegetables or fruits or nuts which are anyways the best possible healthy foods.

Now that we have taken care of what to eat, we need to set a routine as to when to eat. The 16/8 intermittent fasting diet routine has been the most popular form widely recommended unanimously by most health centers and spiritual ashrams from various school of thoughts in different parts of the world. This process of diet clock allows our body to get adequate time for healing and repairing our system. Breakfast at 10 am, lunch at 1 pm, snack at 4pm and dinner at 6 pm serves great for many. You can finetune according to your work schedule and routine, keeping in mind to leave a gap of 16 hours between dinner to next day breakfast.

****

Also, according to an old saying by Adelle Davis — **'Eat breakfast like a king, *lunch like a prince, and dinner like a pauper.'*[5]**

✻✻✻✻✻✻✻✻✻✻✻✻✻✻✻✻✻✻✻✻✻✻✻✻✻✻✻✻✻✻✻✻✻✻✻✻✻

This helps us in regulating our plate size or the quantity of our food. Sunrise to Sunset is the perfect time frame within which we should consume our food. If we follow the food habit of other animals like birds or jungle animals, we will realize that is exactly what they do.

In today's world of abundance let us be careful that our greatest blessings should not turn into our greatest curse. Balance is the Key and scarcity and minimalistic lifestyle in our diet will not only cut down on our hospital bills but also keep us energetic, fit and in shape. Who does not agree with me here that a healthy person is always a better performer with greater productivity and hence have a greater and faster growth and success in his career? A reading tip to all those people in the leadership position is to go through the following course.

[5] https://www.goodreads.com/quotes/87390-eat-breakfast-like-a-king-lunch-like-a-prince-and

("Improving Your Business Through a Culture of Health | Harvard University")[6]

We have got a fair amount of information on the food and diet for our body. Can you guess what is the food for our Mind? Knowingly or unknowingly we often use a phrase- "Food for thought" followed by some idea to ponder upon. Yes, you got it perfectly right. Our mind craves for knowledge and information. If you feed your mind with the right kind of knowledge you get immense satisfaction and happiness. It is quite similar to having a well-balanced diet for your body. When I say "Right" kind of knowledge, that is the most important point to be careful about. What is right and what should be avoided? Anything that gives us knowledge and information and educates us is good so far as there is no trace of negative emotions or news associated with that. When we are

[6] https://online-learning.harvard.edu/course/improving-your-business-through-culture-health?delta=0

studying or researching on a topic or subject for educational purpose it's great. If we are gathering information or upgrading ourselves on topic related to our hobbies or passion- wonderful. What implication do you feel can media, news and newspaper have on our minds? Not desirable. It is said that any news or information that disturbs our mind should be avoided at all means, unless it is unavoidable and concerning your close ones. We need to have full control on our thoughts, on what we think and what we are forced to think by the people around us. I will take this opportunity to bring forth certain quotes and saying by some very wise and famous people as a "food for your thought" so that you can connect well to what I am trying to prove.

****

"We are what we think. All that we are arises with our thoughts. With our thoughts, we make the world." – Buddha[7]

****

Mahatma Gandhi said, ***"Bura mat dekho, bura mat suno, bura mat bolo"*** translated to English "See no evil, hear no evil, speak no evil"[8]

****

There are several occasions when we consume negative food for thought which is really unhealthy for our mind. We need to pick and choose on what thoughts to pay attention on and allow entry in our mind. This is very important and crucial to our mental well-being. Otherwise, the negative thoughts hijack our mind in any unusual circumstances. If some family member misses the usual home coming time and does not reach home without any information, and is for

---

[7] https://www.goodreads.com/quotes/1349139-we-are-what-we-think-all-that-we-are-arises

[8] https://www.quora.com/Why-did-Gandhiji-say-Bura-mat-dekho-bura-mat-suno-bura-mat-bolo-instead-of-acchha-dekho-acchha-bolo-acchha-suno

some reason uncontactable, what happens? Our mind starts getting preoccupied with all the terrible things that could have happened. The reality may be that his phone charge got drained or maybe the phone was left behind at the office work desk by mistake and maybe he realized midway and went back to office to collect it again and hence got delayed. I am sure many of you must have experienced such situations and can relate to what I am saying.

Lot of us try various diet plan and cut on their food to look thirty at fifty. There is nothing bad in that. But we should not try to fix the same goal for our mind. We should not stop feeding our mind at thirty and stop learning. The learning capacity curve as we all know decreases with age. What happens when we stop giving proper food to our mind? The first impact is that we tend to become negative. We all have heard this – ***"An idle brain is the devil's workshop."*** Second, if we stop learning we stop growing in our personal as well as professional life. This happens because we tend to lose pace with the fast-growing society and gradually lose our flexibility and adaptability. We tend to lose track of the ever-growing technology and fail to stay updated and become outdated. Third, since our learnability decreases as we slow down with age the probability of getting Alzheimer's disease increases. So, keep learning and keep your brain engaged and see how Happy You become. Knowledge keeps our mind young and make us feel young. So next time when you make an effort to look 30 at 50, do check out that you are not merely trying to maintain your physical youth but also taking adequate action to keep yourself mentally young. This is the key to a Happy Youthful Life.

****

"It is health that is the real wealth, and not pieces of gold and silver." – Mahatma Gandhi[9]

---

[9]https://in.pinterest.com/pin/392446555004263055/

4. Body-Mind Yoga:

To strengthen the body's muscles, exercise; the mind's muscles, read; the heart's muscles, laugh; and the soul's muscles, love.[10] -by Matshona Dhliwayo

****

There are several forms of Yoga to maintain the wellbeing of your body, soul and spirit.

If there are separate diet for body and mind, you must be wondering whether there will be separate yoga for mind and body. If you pay attention to your body you will often experience that there are several occasions when our body responds physically to our thoughts generated in our mind.

---

[10] https://www.goodreads.com/quotes/8614498-to-strengthen-the-body-s-muscles-exercise-the-mind-s-muscles-read

Let us have a quick check to confirm whether your body is connected to your mind too?

Focus with all your mind and imagine the following actions that are being suggested. Think that you are in your kitchen. You take out a beautiful green juicy lemon from your fridge and bring it on the kitchen table. Take a knife and cut it into two halves. Take one half and squeeze a few drops of the lemon into your mouth. How do you feel?
Have you noticed that even your imagination in your mind could trigger your salivary glands to salivate and make your body ready for the lemon?

This is one example to show how your body is connected to your mind. There are so many examples that happens in our daily life. Have you ever experienced butterflies in your stomach before you have to talk in front of public? Have you ever had goose bumps when you thought of something scary? Have you ever had difficulty in sleeping before your exams or before your first date or say before your interview? There can be a long list of situations where we have all felt such connections.

Now on the reverse side have you ever experienced how your mind responds to your body? If you are not keeping well you tend to be irritated and in a bad mood. Similarly, have you noticed how you feel after a rigorous exercise regime? Do you feel tired after that rigorous exercise or energetic with a great lift in your mood? Have you wondered how can we possibly feel energetic after a rigorous Gym? Strange isn't it? But wait a minute, which type are you? If you are exercising happily then no wonder you will be energetic and happy. But if you are being forced to exercise against your will, you will be tired and drained of energy. Simple, and you already know the reason. You are consuming so much energy in using your will power that your will power battery gets discharged. Here also the list may be long. Do whatever you enjoy at work or at study or at home, you will lose track of time and enjoy, and your energy never decreases but stays intact. The moment you engage yourself in doing something that you are doing simply to satisfy others and not enjoying yourself, you end up draining your energy battery and get tired. Just imagine people you are associated with say your family, friends or colleagues at work. Can you associate with anyone who is always happy, smiling, enjoying what he or she is doing and is fully energetic even after a full day's work? He/ She is the one we would all like to be like. Isn't it?

Is it possible to be like that person? The answer to
this is partly yes. Let me first tell you why I am using Partly yes and what is the cause of Partly No. The reason why sometimes it becomes difficult for us to achieve that state is if we are doing some job which we do not like but doing it simply because we have a family to run and we need money or are not skilled or confident enough to

think that we can opt for the job that matches our skill and passion. Believe me in that scenario only two things can improve your situation. Either leave the job and find yourself a job that you enjoy. Or Incorporate things of your likings in your present job which keeps you engaged and motivated. I have discussed about this in detail in my earlier book, "Happiness GYM".

Now talking about the GYM part which makes it easier for us to have our mind body and spirit not only connected but aligned is YOGA & MEDITATION. Everyone is aware of the benefits of yoga on our physical body. There is also a huge benefit of Yoga on our mind or soul and spirit. It calms and composes our mind and bring stability of thoughts. Your decision making and problem-solving capability reaches to a height. It makes you positive and energetic and keeps your battery charged. It helps reduce your mind wanderings and reduces the streaming of millions of thoughts that otherwise occupy your mind. By doing so it improves your focus, and helps you bc present in the moment. This is what is popularly called mindfulness. Being mindful boosts your performance and productivity in whatever you do, at home or in workplace or education. It boosts your confidence level and paves the pathway to success. One very important evidence that has come forward as a result of medical research is that Yoga and Meditation increases Gray matter. [11]("How Yoga Changes Your Brain - Yoga Medicine." *Yoga Medicine*, 25 Apr. 2019.) According to the study discussed in the journal, our brains have two types of tissues: white and gray matter. We usually have about 60% white matter and 40% gray matter. Gray matter consists of neurons. While it's called gray matter, in reality, it is pink in color. That's because blood continuously flows through it. It turns gray after we die. Due to its

---

[11] https://yogamedicine.com/how-yoga-changes-your-brain/.

concentration of neurons, gray matter is responsible for many of the brain's functions, including learning skills and memory. It is also responsible for the functionality of interpreting senses of sight, hearing, smell, and touch. Additionally, it affects muscle control and self-awareness. It is seen that with volume of gray matter a person's intelligence increases. White matter, on the other hand, are the connections that extend from your brain cells. Its job is to connect different sections of your brain, much like how the internet interconnects the world, by allowing areas of your brain to send and receive signals to one another. As such, healthy white matter allows your brain to coordinate your thoughts as well as your movements.

In general, both gray and white matter complement one another to allow you to think, coordinate movement, and interpret the world surrounding you. Yoga makes you self-aware. It increases your decision-making capability and helps you improve your will power and be more willing to delay gratification. There was a very famous experiment the Marshmallow exercise to get an idea on why delayed gratification can be helpful which I will describe in a while. Yoga also increases the folds in the brain and hence has the capacity to accommodate more brain cells, thus increasing the surface area of the brain and hence holds more neurons. According to a study by UCLA researchers, MRI brain scans showed that meditation practices increases the gyrification or the number of folds in brain. 20 years or more of meditation practice significantly increased the gyrifications in the cerebral cortex. Since the cerebral cortex is responsible for language, reasoning, perception, information processing, memory, and voluntary movement, the increase in gyrification allows for better functioning and faster information processing. During yoga, the brain releases certain chemicals that not only help you relax but also lower your stress and anxiety levels. It releases gamma-aminobutyric acid (GABA), dopamine, oxytocin, serotonin, and endorphins. Each of these chemicals' functions in its own way to help you calm down and feel Happier. During Yoga certain parts of the brain the frontal lobe and the parietal lobe part of the brain slows and calms down and hence helps to de-stress. Stress is in itself a good thing as it prepares the body to face uncertain situations and help to deal with the situation. The body releases stress hormones to help you become more alert, make your heart beat faster, and spike your blood pressure. All of these are a result of your body getting flooded by stress hormones including cortisol and adrenaline. However, if stress is sustained for long or is habitual then the side effects are worse. Release of more sugar into your bloodstream, increase in your blood pressure, and inflammation are some of the side effects of prolonged stress. When sustained for long periods of time, this can result in serious conditions like heart disease, high blood pressure, and diabetes. Yoga helps to reverse these effects. Yoga reduces stress by lowering your body's cortisol and adrenaline levels, two critical stress hormones.

Yoga Controls Ageing and keeps you Young and Energetic. Research says that our DNA strands become longer with regular Meditation, which increases our lifespan. With multifold benefits of yoga on your mind and body you can gain full control of these two very powerful tools that we possess to make our life blissful and ecstatic.

****

"A good laugh and a long sleep are the best cures in the doctor's book." – Irish proverb (Emmy Lymn) [12]

****

---

[12] https://philosophyvia.photos/2019/02/23/a-good-laugh-and-a-long-sleep-are-the-best-cures-in-the-doctors-book-irish-proverb/

Holistic yoga consists of three main components that improves your physical, mental, and spiritual wellbeing. These come in the form of the asanas, breathwork or pranayama, and meditation.

Let us imagine a story. There was an office in Washington in which the sales department was being headed by Samuel with junior sales representatives Mac, Williams, Emeka and Ben reporting to him. Samuel was a very generous and considerate leader and always allowed the junior team to work according to their choice and preference. Mac was very moody. Every now & then he used to be upset with something or the other. A very common dialogue was. "I am upset." Ben on the other hand was very irregular to work and complained of health issues. So, most of the time his work used to get piled up and a lot of time Mac, Emeka and Williams had to do extra work to compensate for the undone job of Ben. Mac used to get stressed because of this and they used to have a lot of arguments and clashes. At times the clashes used to get so strong that Williams had to come in to resolve their fights. Emeka was a person who was very adaptable. He used to behave as per the prevailing situation and did not generally have an opinion of his own. One thing was common in all and that was that each one acted as per their own preference. They lacked a routine, a set process or a discipline. Now can you guess what was the performance of the branch as compared to other branches? The answer is quite obvious, without a process and discipline anything and everything will fall out of place. That is exactly what happened. The branch was rated as a poor performing branch. Can you guess whose fault is this? What would you have done had you been in Samuel's place? Let me take this story a little forward. After a few months, the company's CEO called upon Samuel and asked him how he proposes to improve the performance of the branch and what are the root causes of his failure to exhibit a growth. Samuel was disturbed and tried to defend himself by pointing out the problems what is stopping him to be successful. The CEO told him to act like a King and take full control of his team and be strict with them. He asked him to have a disciplined approach as a team leader and do a regular review with his team to track if the team is acting as a ONE and all the members are completely aligned towards the only ONE THING, their GOAL, The TARGET. He told Samuel to be Focused on only one objective and not to consider any excuses for non-performance. What do you think happened after a month? Yes, they achieved their target. The team behaved as one entity. The clashes ccased to exist and they worked in complete cohesion and collaboration. They worked happily. Their performance and productivity increased immensely.

In this story, let us replace the characters and see what happens.

Samuel is the "I" in us. The spirit. Mac, the mind; Williams, the Will; Emeka, the Emotions in us; Ben, our body. Now if you again read the story, you realize why we fall short of success? The reason is mostly because we don't have control over our mind and body. I, the leader, the king, the owner gives in to the demands of the mind and body and instead of controlling them allow the mind or the body to have the power and control the "I," The Spirit. All the internal clashes hinder our performance and productivity and acts as big hurdles in our road to success. We fail and then start pointing out at others or situations, for our failures. This blame-game stops us from introspecting and identifying the reasons responsible for our failure and we get stressed as we feel that we are not able to control our fate.

The key to ultimate wellness and happiness is if our soul mind and body coexist in a harmonious way.[13]

("Soul Mind and Body") Attaining this balance should be an important goal for every individual on earth today. We however mostly do not pay heed to his basic functioning and collaboration between our internal attributes and lead a life full of internal conflict. These CLASHES manifests through several mental, emotional and physical ailments.

****

"Those who think they have no time for exercise will sooner or later have to find time for illness." —[14]("Edward Stanley #quote… | Fitness Motivation, Exercise, Fitness")

****

---

[13] https://www.trivedieffect.com/inspiration-blog/soul-mind-and-body/

[14] https://www.pinterest.co.uk/pin/13581236360887493/

5. Our Body:

To keep the body in good health is a duty, otherwise we shall not be able to keep our mind strong and clear." –Buddha Quotes[15]("Health Quotes for a Healthy Body, Mind, and Soul | – YourSelfQuotes.Com")

****

We have already discussed, that the physiological body is the physical or the material part of us on earth. The Body that we possess is a means given to our spirit to communicate to the outer world by using the five senses of sight, smell, taste, touch, and hearing. When our body works aligned to the mind and spirit, we are in harmony and experience peace and bliss and are successful. Disease occurs when the mind, body and soul are not working in harmony, the term dis-ease represents the turmoil created when these three components are out

---

[15] https://www.yourselfquotes.com/health-quotes-for-body-mind-soul/

of alignment. When we are not at ease, we have a disease. The Human Body happens to be the most complex machine on earth designed to serve our soul and spirit. It is composed of 50 trillion cells of which the organs, bones, tissue, and all our body systems and parts are made of. However, the complex machine that we have for our use should be in our control and be used to fulfil our goals and achieve the purpose of our life. One example will make this concept easier to understand. Suppose we have to go to a certain destination. We sit in our automated car. The car instead of taking instruction from us starts acting on its own will and starts moving and takes us to a different destination. How will you feel? You will feel strange and find it difficult to understand. You feel how can that be possible, isn't it? This is exactly what is happening for most of us in our present life. We fail to understand the meaning and purpose of this life or the destiny of the spirit. Our two most powerful tools or weapons which are meant to serve our spirit to attain our destiny, instead of taking guidance and instruction from us, the spirit, act according to their own desires and will and makes life complicated, unfit, full of suffering and pain. We need to understand our true self and take full control of our body and make it act as per our directions so that we can reach our goal and have a blissful life.

Many of us spend a huge fortune on outfits, jewelry and beauty products desperately trying to look gorgeous. The amount of money and more importantly time must be used wisely. Looking good is definitely important in todays world but can we take some time to increase the inner harmony and beauty of ourselves just by practicing a few GYM activities as a daily regime.

****

"Every living cell in your body is made from the food you eat. If you consistently eat junk food then you'll have a junk body." —[16](

"Jeanette Jenkins - Greatest Physiques")

****

A. Daily GYM for a Healthy Body:

1. Proper Nutrition & Diet Consumption.
2. Follow a Healthy Lifestyle and Cleanliness Regime.
3. Regular Meditation & Exercise. Practice Staying Calm, Cheerful & Happy.

****

"Early to bed and early to rise, makes a man healthy wealthy and wise." — [17]Benjamin Franklin

****

---

[16] https://www.greatestphysiques.com/female-physiques/jeanette-jenkins/

[17] https://www.brainyquote.com/quotes/benjamin_franklin_564198

6. Our Soul:

Our soul is what gives us our personality. Soul is not physical and cannot be seen, it is intangible but is a reality and is believed to be immortal like the spirit. Our soul is believed to have three parts- our mind, will and emotions. Our mind has a conscious part, a subconscious part and an unconscious part. The conscious mind is the logical part of our brain where we do our thinking and reasoning. The sub-conscious mind is where we hold our deep beliefs and our attitudes. It's also where we have our feeling, our emotions and retain our memories. The unconscious mind consists of the processes in the mind which occur automatically and are not available to introspection and include thought processes, memories, interests and motivations. Our will is what gives us the ability to make choices. Through a very complex way, our mind, our will and our emotions are connected to the body through our endocrine, nervous and immune systems.[18] ("Spirit Mind Body Health – A Christian Perspective on God's Design of Man")

Today as we are gearing up our lives with the Industrial Revolution 4.0 let us try to create an analogy of ourselves with the digital machine.[19] (Computer Science analogy for your Body, Mind and Soul Dhanraj Acharya)

****

"Physical fitness is not only one of the most important keys to a healthy body it is the basis of dynamic and creative intellectual activity." [20] (John F. Kennedy · MindZip")

---

[18] https://www.faithandhealthconnection.org/the_connection/spirit-soul-and-body/

[19] https://medium.com/@dhanraj_acharya/computer-science-analogy-for-your-body-mind-and-soul-807a2f87228d

[20] https://in.pinterest.com/pin/314477986451349175/

****

7. Our Mind:

Just like the computer or laptop or the digital machine is composed of physical hardware components and the machine functions effectively if all the hardware components are working efficiently, similarly we human beings are composed of physical matter and our bones, muscles, nerves, organs can be considered as the interconnected hardware parts. If all our body parts are functioning efficiently, we are healthy and we function smoothly. However, the computer does not work even if all hardware components are in proper order unless we have an operating system installed in it. Similar to the OS is our Soul. Without soul, the body doesn't function. Mind is compared to the processor. The mind is responsible for generating thoughts, and is the source of intelligence and reasoning. The mind influences our actions and emotions and is manifested as our behaviors and attitude. The conscious part of the mind is compared with the volatile memory or the RAM which is also called Random Access Memory. The conscious memory in a human body is not functioning when a person sleeps but its subconscious part become super active in the sleep stage. The subconscious mind is usually compared with the Hard Disc or storage which stores the memory. This is the vital part that we need to focus on which is most active when we are preparing to sleep or just wake up from sleep. At that time our subconscious mind comprises more than 90% of our mind and hence this is the time when we should be doing all the positive thinking, affirmations, positive visualization, meditation practices and chanting mantras or listening to devotional songs or read sacred books or focus on spiritual speeches. This is the powerful segment which we ignore most of the times. It has been found that if we want to pick up a new language, it is very useful to play an audio in a soft tune in that language while we go to sleep listening to the language. If done for quite some time, the subconscious mind is capable of learning the new language fast. Whatever we do, see, listen habitually and quite often, goes to our subconscious mind. The mind does not differentiate if it is the positive or negative but stores it as an image in the subconscious mind and produces it whenever needed. So, we need to pick and choose what we are filling our subconscious mind with. In computer analogy we use the terms automation and artificial intelligence or AI as it is popularly called, almost everywhere now a days. We use automation in the latest cars or many IOT devices. A major task of our subconscious mind is automation.

✳✳✳✳✳✳✳✳✳✳✳✳✳✳✳✳✳✳✳✳✳✳✳✳✳✳✳✳✳✳✳✳✳✳✳

B. A Do-It-Yourself Mind GYM:

Think of the tasks that you do from the time you wake up till the time you go to bed. Write them down in your self-study journal. Recording should be in "Day- time- activity" format. Repeat this process for at least 10 days. Do not miss out any task even if it appears obvious like brushing your teeth, combing your hair, drinking a cup of tea. Detailed entry is recommended. Highlight the tasks that you see are habitual and done on a daily basis. Most of the time you will find a sequence is maintained and a timeliness or routine pattern is maintained for people who have a disciplined approach towards life. For others the time may alter but there also the sequence pattern is similar. You will be surprised to know that the more automated our responses become, less will power is utilized and less energy is used up. Even after doing lot of work we feel highly energetic if we are having most of the tasks done automatically by our subconscious mind. Anything that we do on a regular part form a part of our subconscious mind. Here I must mention, if we think about something on a daily basis, that thought also gets registered in our subconscious mind. That is the reason we are taught to stay away from negative information, incidence, environment or people. The more we stay associated with negative minded people the more of that culture we start acquiring. This is the reason why we ask our children to make good friends and stay away from bad people while sending them to school or playgrounds. Today we have access to both the good and bad through our smart phones and social media and that is exactly the reason why we need to be cautious in using social media so that it can help us and take us towards fulfilment & happiness rather than the opposite. In a similar fashion it is important to keep on saying positive affirmation statements in a way as if we have already achieved what we want to achieve. A daily gratitude affirmation practice where we say to ourselves that we are gratefully experiencing the benefits of what we want in our lives coupled with positive visualization exercises work like magic and makes us achieve our Goals faster. Recommended reading or viewing[21] is the book named "power of Subconscious Mind by Joseph Murphy". It's said the average person makes 35,000 decisions every day[22](Bloem). A simple way to save brain power is to cut down on the number of decisions you need to make. You will be surprised to know that some of the world's most successful people have chosen to

---

[21]https://www.youtube.com/watch?v=BLEYCyrLpkI&t=1368s

[22] https://www.inc.com/craig-bloem/this-1-unusual-habit-helped-make-mark-zuckerberg-steve-jobs-dr-dre-successful.html

wear the same work outfit daily. "I really want to clear my life to make it so that I have to make as few decisions as possible about anything except how to best serve this community," Zuckerberg said during a 2014 Q&A session.[23] (Wener-Fligner)

He clarified though that he has multiple same shirts.   Mark Zuckerberg in jeans and a gray t-shirt, Steve Jobs' iconic black turtleneck. Even people like Barack Obama and Michael Kors wear the same or similar outfits every day. This has been done deliberately to reduce the number of decisions that they have to take otherwise daily in the morning. The fact is that every day we simply have to use our energy in deciding on what to wear, what to eat for breakfast, which vehicle to take to office, what lunch to carry and so on and by the time when we reach office and we are required to take important decisions we get to feel decision

[23] https://qz.com/292993/why-mark-zuckerberg-wears-the-same-teeshirt-every-day/

fatigue.[24] Find out which are the areas that you need to take decision on a daily basis and work on setting a routine or pattern so that you too can save on decision making and make it into a habit that will be automated by the subconscious mind. Basically, the job of our subconscious mind is to trigger responses exactly as we are programmed to respond. Our brain retrieves the data from the storage or memory bank and responds to a situation. The Subconscious mind does not think logically or rationally. Only our conscious mind has the ability to think logically. The subconscious mind can be trained by our conscious mind through repeated and habitual positive affirmations, visualization, motivational actions, inspirational quotes, positive actions thus forming a habit so that it can act on the auto-pilot mode thus saving time and energy which is otherwise required in decision

[24] https://rentwear.com/work-uniforms-relieve-stress/

making. All your habits and actions get stored in the subconscious mind. This is also a reason why when we are required to do anything new, we often resist moving out of our comfort zone. We realize, in this case, the subconscious mind is actually responsible for pulling us behind, to stay in our comfort zone, every time we are needed to start something new. Here the technique that successful people utilize is to train the mind to form a habit of doing or learning something new as a part of Habit that keeps pushing the person out of their comfort zone.[25]

****

C. *Daily GYM for a Healthy Mind:*

---

[25] https://www.briantracy.com/blog/personal-success/understanding-your-subconscious-mind/

1. Practice Gratitude
2. Practice Positive Affirmations & Visualization Exercises for achieving your specific Life Goal.
3. Brain Exercises with Quiz & Puzzles
4. Regular Upgradation of Knowledge through Learning.
5. Leading a Happiness Lifestyle
6. Be Compassionate to Others
7. Practice Mindfulness Meditation

****

8. Our Will Power:

"Our bodies are our gardens to the which our wills are gardeners." — William Shakespeare, Othello[26] ("Body Quotes & Sayings (Our Bodies, Anatomy, Blood, Health, Wellness, Body Awareness, Nudity, Etc)")

****

The Will Power[27] also plays a vital role in helping the person to move out of comfort zone and acquire new habits of accepting or abandoning certain things which will be helpful in the long run.

The dictionary meaning of the word Will-Power is determination, self-discipline, self-control, self-regulation, effortful control.

---

[26] https://www.quotegarden.com/body.html

[27] https://positivepsychology.com/psychology-of-willpower/

We may think of will power as the judge who supports the mind or the body depending on situations whenever there is a clash between mind and body. According to APA (American Psychological Association), most psychology researchers define willpower as: ("The Psychology of Willpower: Training the Brain for Better Decisions")

- The ability to delay gratification and resist short-term temptations to meet long-term goals;
- The capacity to override an unwanted thought, feeling or impulse;
- The conscious, effortful regulation of the self, by the self;
- A limited resource capable of being depleted.

I will give few examples to demonstrate:

1. Sight of cigarette makes your body crave for it but mind says no. Will power have to be

exerted for self-regulation for the sake of your health benefit. You need to resist temptation. Same is the case for chocolates or desserts which generates craving in a diabetic patient or any person with a sweet tooth and the mind needs will power to intervene and exert the extra control power to be exerted to check your craving and say no to sweets or cigarettes or excessive alcohol as the case may be. In all these above cases body and five senses say yes and are screaming to have the feeling of pleasure as is recorded in our subconscious mind but logical conscious mind acts against the subconscious mind and body and associates with will power and uses the energy of will to execute its decision.

Psychologist Kelly McGonigal calls this the "I won't power." McGonigal is a frequent lecturer at Stanford University and the author of "The Willpower Instinct." In an experiment performed by Walter Mischel, now a psychologist at Columbia University set out to study self-control in children, with a simple yet effective test called "The Marshmallow Test.[28] (Do watch the video in you tube " The Marshmallow Test") Marshmallow is a very tasty mouthwatering tempting chocolate which is very irresistible. Children were given a marshmallow in front of them in a closed room without any other things like books or toys or friends to engage with. Each child was presented a marshmallow in a plate in front of him and was told that if he could resist having it till the researcher returns then he will get another marshmallow as a reward. So, the result of his delayed gratification will earn him two marshmallows. If he finds it difficult to wait then he

[28]https://www.youtube.com/watch?v=QX_0y9614HQ

can have the one offered in front of him. When followed up for years and 30 years after the first test, it is observed that the children who waited for the second marshmallow during their childhood when the test was conducted, indicated as having higher will power. They were more successful in their studies and career and scored higher in SAT's and had lower BMI-body mass index.

2. There are also situations when the body says "no" but the mind says "Yes". Here too, Will power is needed to support the conscious logical mind against the subconscious experience of pleasure experience by the body. Example when we intend to wake up early in the morning for a morning walk or meditation, but many a times we have a tendency to listen to our body and delay the process by lying down for a little more time. Will here come into action and may actually push us to

wake up listening to our mind. A person with stronger will says yes to getting up but a person with weaker will continues to lie down till late and ignore the mind.

3. There is a third scenario where we need to exert our will on both our conscious mind and our subconscious mind and body. This happens when we intend to achieve some future goal and need to work towards it. Since our subconscious mind do not have any prerecorded experience of pleasure, it resists our body to move out of the comfort zone and habit and opposes the conscious mind. The will here again is needed to come into action and dominate over the subconscious mind and body and say strongly "I want to". A person with stronger will are more likely to be successful in achieving Goals and acquire new habits. As an instance, when we are practicing Positive affirmations and visualizations

our entire thought process is driven by the "I Want to" experience to reach what "I want in my Life" or "the Goal".

Willpower according to McGonigal is comprised of three things:

- I won't power;
- I will power;
- I want power (remembering what you really want).

In any event whenever the two dimensions are in conflict, will power is the parameter which decides which will win. When will power is strong and desire loses person is more likely to succeed. When desire overpowers will power the person is weaker in executing the actions that will be logically beneficial and would take him towards his goal. In this scenario the person fails to become successful.

****

"The biggest enemies of willpower: temptation, self-criticism, and stress. (...) these three skills —self-awareness, self-care, and remembering what matter most— are the foundation for self-control." — Kelly McGonigal, The Willpower Instinct: How Self-Control Works, Why It Matters, and What You Can Do to Get More of It.[29]

****

Will Power Inhibitors: Stress, Temptation and Desire, Self-criticism and Guilt acts as inhibitors against exerting our will power. For example, sight of desserts or cigarettes releases dopamine and this in turn increases our tendency to give in to instant gratification rather than self-control for long-term benefits.

---

[29]https://www.goodreads.com/work/quotes/1755351 4-the-willpower-instinct-how-self-control-works-why-it-matters-and-what

****

D. Will Power Strengthening Gym:

Gym Activities that help us develop and strengthen our Will Power are:

1. **Self-awareness and mindfulness**: Each day we are required to take several choices and we need to be aware of what decisions we are taking? It is very important that we understand the What-Why-when-where-how's of decision-making so that we don't rely on the auto-pilot mode based only on how our subconscious mind drives us to act or think or feel. Keep a record in your journal of what all things you have done in a day and then do a self-review and analysis of whether your decision or choice was based on long term goal achievement or was it to satisfy your desire or instant gratification. This activity helps in reflecting on our decision making and trains our mind gradually to do a check occasionally before we act.

Remember we had mentioned that the subconscious mind cannot differentiate between good or bad and act on the basis of what auto responses are generated by triggers. This self-analysis helps us to have a check on how we are responding to the external stimuli.

2. **Exercise**: Megan Oaten and Ken Cheng devised a study of treatment to enhance self-control. The participants were 6 men and 18 women, ages 18-50. After two months of treatment in form of exercise in Gym these people were:

- Eating less junk food;
- Eating more healthy foods;
- Watching less television;
- Studying more;
- Saving more money;
- Procrastinating less;
- Arriving more on time to appointments.

Any type of physical exercise and/or outdoor exercises increases will power in an individual. The bullets are also very much indicative of what we should strive to achieve and what is good for us to prioritize.

3. **Meditation**: Regular meditators have more gray matter in the prefrontal cortex of the brain that is responsible for self-awareness.

4. **Healthy Eating**: Will power is like a battery. It gets depleted with usage. Just like we charge our mobile and start the day with a full charge. As the day passes with usage the battery gets drained of the energy and the charge lowers. Same is the case with will power. We start our day with high level of will power but gradually as the day progresses it gets depleted. When we exert considerable amount of will power our fuel for the body-glucose gets depleted and this alerts our brain and triggers our body to release sugar to make up for the fall in blood sugar. This leads to sugar craving. High level of sugar on the other hand is also not desirable. High sugar content in blood increases stress levels and hence our will power becomes weak. So, it is

highly advisable to have a well balance diet.

5. **Relaxation**: Sleep, relaxation exercises like pranayama, yoga, a pleasant walk, praying, listening to music, reading books, getting a massage, spending time with friends and family are great will power boosting activities. This helps people to be able to control stress, delay gratification and stay focused by ignoring cravings and distractions.

****

"If freedom is short of weapons, we must compensate with willpower." [30] — Adolf Hitler

****

---

[30] https://www.goodreads.com/quotes/218561-if-freedom-is-short-of-weapons-we-must-compensate-with. Accessed 10 Jan. 2021.

9. Our Emotion:

"I don't want to be at the mercy of my emotions. I want to use them, to enjoy them, and to dominate them."
— Oscar Wilde, The Picture of Dorian Gray.[31]

****

This is that aspect of our soul that bridges the mind and the body and is considered to be the language of the soul. The feelings and emotions help us manifest and communicate to the outer world.

Whatever thoughts arise in our mind it gets communicated to the body through our emotions and becomes visible to others and external world through our physical response system. Whatever is manifested by our physiological body is a

---

[31] https://quotecatalog.com/quote/oscar-wilde-i-dont-want-to-vpZDR41

communication of our emotions that arise from the thought generated.

The response system associated with a happy feeling or any positive feeling is good and does not require any form of intervention as it is naturally taking care of our well-being. The problem arises when we have a negative thought in our mind. We get exposed to a negative thought either when we ourselves generate or come across in the external world or we feed our mind with a negative piece of information. I agree there are unavoidable situations when we simply can't stay away from a negative scenario or information but we have an option to avoid in most situations. Why does it become a concern when we have a negative thought? A negative emotion triggers rise of cortisol levels and also weakens our immune system with time. Constant negative state of mind gradually drains us of our energy and creates dis-ease in our body. We become more prone to pains and aches in our body and as a result are more likely to be in an irritable mood, less likely to interact socially and focus more on the pain than pay attention to self-care and self- compassion. When such repeated occurrence of negative thoughts and emotions becomes the norm, our overall well-being is negatively affected and our happiness becomes restricted.

E.   *Emotion Strengthening Gym:*

Mindfulness Meditation is the best way to handle this problem. Being mindful of your emotions, studying and observing carefully of what kinds of thoughts and information triggers the negative emotions in you over a period of time will enable you to learn to come up with a solution. Train yourself to look out for the trigger situations and avoid them or even in case if you come across the trigger situation, pause and take time to accept the situation being fully aware that the situation will pass and things will improve, before you react negatively. Take a dcep breath and observe and analyze and come up with a best possible solution.

****

"But feelings can't be ignored, no matter how unjust or ungrateful they seem." — [32]Anne Frank, The Diary of a Young Girl

****

"Your emotions are the slaves to your thoughts, and you are the slave to your emotions." — [33](Quote by Elizabeth Gilbert, Eat Pray Love: One Woman's Search for Everything Across Italy, India and Indonesia - QuotesLyfe")

---

[32] https://www.goodreads.com/quotes/431935-but-feelings-can-t-be-ignored-no-matter-how-unjust-or

[33] https://www.quoteslyfe.com/quote/Your-emotions-are-the-slaves-to-your-1942

****

10.   Our Spirit:

"A man's spirit is free, but his pride binds him with chains of suffocation in a prison of his own insecurities" — Jeremy Aldana[34]

****

It's in our spirit that we have meaning and purpose in life. It is believed to be eternal. It is existing in the form of energy that connects us to Divinity. The spirit can be compared to the cloud technology in technical terminology or the virtual workspace which can be accessed from another machine even if the computer crashes or gets out of order. Similarly, even when our body ceases to exist, the spiritual energy continues to exist and can be accessed by another life as the spirit moves on to its next birth. Some people function predominantly by focusing on their Body, some focuses

---

[34] https://www.goodreads.com/quotes/380805-a-man-s-spirit-is-free-but-his-pride-binds-him

on Mind and some are on the Spiritually Active level. Today greater and greater numbers of people suffer from stress disorder, anxiety, depression, fear of the future, boredom, low confidence and are unhappy in their lives. It is time that people start to recognize and connect with their inner guidance system get back into balance, following their own natural instinct that is right for them rather than leading a compromised life directed towards satisfying the standards set by others and pressures created by society. Our Spirit is the true nature of self. If we treat the spirit within us as the Guardian and owner of our mind and body and listen to what our inner voice says, we are most likely to live a Happy and Successful Life.

The Sixth Sense or The Guardian:
Analogy Story of Parenting:

For a clear realization let us again take the example of a family. While telling the story I will be drawing an analogy with the system that we are housing internally within us. The head of the family here is the mother, The Spirit. The mother gives birth to a twin, named Mind and Body. At birth both mind and body are divinely connected to their mother, Spirit and since they do not have any experience as new born, they rely mostly on their intuitions. A new born needs no training to be able to suckle milk from mother and no one tells them to cry when they need to draw attention. The universal intelligence guides them to do so. From this stage they start learning depending on the kind of attention and response that they receive from the world. Every time they face a new situation, they try to deal with it through intuition and then depending on their intuitive actions they receive responses which are either desirable or undesirable and they create and store the memories formed in memory banks for future references when needed. Next time if they face similar situations they will act and behave depending on the outcome of the previous experience. If the outcome gave them pleasure, they will repeat, if otherwise, they will take a step back due to fear. In an orphanage room having more than 50 babies in cots, surprisingly it was seen that no one was crying and there was a striking silence. On enquiry it was learnt that the babies did not cry even when they were hungry because they were not attended to and responded when they signaled and communicated their hunger by their intuitive response of crying. Slowly their subconscious mind learnt that crying will not be responded by fulfilling their needs and then they gave up. With each passing instances the memory bank grows stronger and stronger with experiences. As the memory bank storage goes up, the children gradually lose connection with their intuition and start to behave and respond to the external stimulus through their memory bank experiences. Now that body and mind gradually distance from the spirit and start living life as per their experiences. It is quite apparent that the two will behave differently at times and gain and gather different experiences. Hence situations at home arises that though brought up in the same family and environment two siblings have a very varied system of response towards similar choices. Even in case of twins we often find completely different behavior and attitude as each one has a pattern set in subconscious part of their brain depending on their experiences of pain or pleasure. Now imagine a scenario where the mother is quite strict and disciplined and guides the body and mind continuously so that the body and mind both are only experiencing situations and require to act intuitively based on a common universal divine guideline set by the Mother, Spirit. In this scenario, the actions taken by the children will be more aligned and the family will be Happier with no possibility of internal conflict. There will be a harmony existing between the Spirit, mind and body and will experience a life of well-being and fulfilment. If the mother sets the rule that choosing food for the body will be based on dietary needs for the body and no sugar must be consumed and diet should be predominantly fresh vegetables and fruits, then there will be no chance of interference by the body or mind to have any clash. The body does not get a chance to crave for chocolates and the mind does not get a chance to take any logical support for the body to consume the chocolate or even develop a logic against the chocolate and develop a clash with the body. Best part is the Will does not have to be exercised as that action is already taken care of proactively when the guideline was prepared based on the needs of the body and mind. Here the body and mind act like obedient children and the Spirit guides what is right for the body and mind. Just like the mother knows best when to give what for her children, the Spirit knows best what is right for the body and mind. It is always better to take help of situation support when trying to train our mind and body and trying to align them with mind. We can create environment in our kitchen where we keep the healthy fruits and vegetables and nuts open to sight and within our easy reach to encourage ourselves to choose them for to satisfy our hunger. We can keep cookies and chocolates and candy or chips and coffee away from our sight and if possible, away from our homes. This way we can design for any task that we would like ourselves to do and create favorable situation support for the same. Keep the meditation music set up in the morning that goes on automatically in place of alarm and keep the Yoga mattress right in front to pull ourselves out of bed. You can even keep the alarm clock out of your reach so that when it rings you are bound to step out of bed to put it off. Think of any task and create such situations that support our plan of action. Gradually you get into a habit and then one day you will no longer require such situation support. With religious habits you start reaping the benefits. We should look for places and situations where we can trigger automated responses which is aligned to our mind and body and is favorable for us.

Similarly, you all are aware that even the very disciplined families have certain grants and relaxation based on certain occasions or requirements. And children from very strict families also indulge in certain activities which may not be following the rule of the family. So being Human a little here and there with mild alterations will definitely not cause any harm as far as the action taken is not likely to be highly disapproved by the divine spirit. For e.g., things like taking drugs or maybe ice-cream for a highly diabetic patient may not be recommended. The key to the success is the balance. We need to understand where to draw the line and we need to respect what our spirit expects from us. I am sure with proper meditation and yoga practice your spirit will guide you on what you should or what you should not. The more you start to realign your body, mind and spirit the more will your intuition be developed. This is what we popularly call as the Sixth Sense. The Sixth sense or our intuition or our gut feeling or guidance by the Spirit, the Higher Self or Soul, God, and consciousness by whatever name we call, we have reduced our access to it as we have become more and more dependent on our five bodily senses now a days. Just like we love the concept of reverse aging and would love to look 30 at 50 years. Can we think of using this concept to look and feel young and genuinely go for a reverse aging procedure, through the regular practice of Yoga and meditation and aligning our body and mind with our spirit? According to Jill Willard an exceptionally gifted L.A.-based intuitive who taught us how to Trust the Gut[35]

Start paying attention to your intuitive feeling and pay attention to what gut feeling you have. Note them down in your GYM Journal. Later revisit the journal to find out how many times your gut feeling gave you the right direction. Gradually your intuition becomes stronger and well

[35] https://goop.com/wellness/spirituality/trust-the-gut-harnessing-intuition/

developed as you gain confidence and learn to rely on your intuitive feeling with more confidence.

Quiet time, experiencing stillness, and taking time to stretch, meditate, walk outside, swim, yoga...these are all very powerful tools.

We need to start living in the moment and enjoy the NOW moment instead of focusing on past memories and future anticipations. We should split our day in such a way that we start to enjoy taking long meals with loved ones, walking, relaxing, and connecting. We need to practice Gratitude for our existence and all that is. We need to be exercising our intuitive power to empower our sixth sense.

****

Albert Einstein once said, ***"The intuitive mind is a sacred gift and the rational mind is a faithful servant. We have created a society that honors*** *the servant and has forgotten the gift."*[36]

****

F. Daily Spiritual Gym

1. Read Spiritual Books
2. Forgive others
3. Practice self-compassion
4. Meditate & Pray
5. Love and serve others
6. Stay in community and be socially connected
7. Write your thoughts in a journal without screening, filtering, analyzing, reasoning or logical interpretation or editing. Revisit and find out how many times your Gut feeling gave you the right guidance.
8. Whenever you are facing a decision-making stage-brainstorm and write down all your ideas. Try to identify

---

[36] https://quoteinvestigator.com/2013/09/18/intuitive-mind/

the one which is in tune with your gut feeling. Remember that our intuition is often wiser and more intelligent and guides us to take the right path. This happens mostly because we are mostly making our decisions based on logic and experience which are limited and bounded by our exposure in the past. This often puts a barrier and limits us to take a decision that puts us in a challenging new scenario out of our comfort zone.

9. Start listening to yourself
10. Live in the present moment
11. Practice Positive Affirmations
12. Practice Positive Visualizations

****

A healthy Spirit is symbolic of realization that he/she is a part of something much bigger than self. Being spiritually healthy includes being part of a community to share yourself with others, and to give without expecting anything tangible in return. There is a need to being loved.

As we begin to understand the answer to "Who am I" is that "I am a Spirit with a certain purpose in Life". We possess the two most powerful tools - the Mind and the Body to fulfil the purpose of this life. We realize that we need to make the best use of these two tools to live a life of fulfilment, bliss and ecstasy.

****

11.   How to balance Body-Soul-Spirit?

We are Spirit, have a soul and live in a body[37]

(Your Way to God through Mind, Body, Soul, and Spirit, updated on November 19, 2020 | Published on September 25, 2019)

****

G. The Total Body-Soul-Spirit Alignment GYM:

The Summary of GYM Activities:
To sum up, we see that in creating a healthy lifestyle and in achieving a harmonious alignment of our body-soul spirit there are few GYM[38] activities which have been mentioned repeatedly. The following list if practiced daily and with conviction

---

[37] https://www.faithandhealthconnection.org/the_connection/spirit-soul-and-body/

[38] https://themindfool.com/pave-your-way-to-god-through-mind-body-soul-and-spirit/

can you train your mind and body to act in coordination and perfect sync.

1. **Meditation Practice enhances your ability to be calm and be a silent observer and enables you to be able to respond to a situation without reacting to it and getting affected in a negative way as the case may be.[39] (Happiness GYM: How to become Successful…By Rajashree Chakraborty)**
2. **Yoga and Pranayama practice.**
3. **Develop a habit of reading a few pages from a Holy book or a book on spirituality daily.**
4. **Listen to music, sing or dance whichever gives you joy as Music is a great way to heal and bring alignment in you.**

---

[39] https://www.amazon.com/dp/B08NZS3Z7J

5. Practice gratefulness and love the nature for its abundance and try to use the nature's gifts in original form and stay connected with the gifts that are given to you. Practice gardening or go for swimming or barefoot walking on grass or mud, use nature fresh fruits and vegetables and sprouts and nuts for your diet. Gratitude is the most important key to your happiness and well-being just after meditation and pranayama.

6. Have a stress-free mind and learn to find time for adequate sleep and rest. It is good at times to go for a spa or a Detox tour for rejuvenation.

7. Take your time to indulge in activities that you love or are passionate about. Practice your hobby or sports without any burden of excelling or winning.

Just get into the flow at intervals to rewind.

8. Be socially connected, generous and forgiving. Be compassionate and kind to all. The energy of Love should flow incessantly from you to the outside world.

9. Have some outdoor activity in the sunshine either in the early morning or in the afternoon around sunset in form of walks, swimming in the open pools, practice some sports or practice yoga, pranayama in the open in the garden or terrace under the sun. Sun bathing helps you in boosting your well-being.

10. Join a new course like a language class or anything that boosts your knowledge. Keep yourself engaged in learning new things.

11. Do not procrastinate and keep piling up your work

for later. A stitch in time saves nine. Also keeping tasks completed as and when it comes within time frame keeps you relaxed and stress free.

12. Make a habit of writing down your dreams and Goals and see it regularly. Practice positive affirmations and visualization of your GOAL daily. Live your goal as if you have already achieved it and precondition your mind and body and align it towards your achieving the goal and see how fast you achieve it.

13. Lead a Healthy Lifestyle

How do you realize when you attain this Spirit-Soul-Body alignment?

When we are in a state of harmony, we experience the following:[40] ("Body,

---

[40] http://sshc.in/?p=1584

Mind and Soul Connection | Health Wellness & Sickness")

1. *Self-awareness*
2. *Realization of life purpose*
3. *Raised consciousness*
4. *No fear of the uncertain*
5. *A deep connection with the God of our belief*
6. *Blissfulness*
7. *Success*

****

"To ensure good health: eat lightly, breathe deeply, live moderately, cultivate cheerfulness, and maintain an interest in life." -William Londen[41](Tiny Buddha)

---

[41] https://tinybuddha.com/wisdom-quotes/to-ensure-good-health-eat-lightly-breathe-deeply-live-moderately-cultivate-cheerfulness-and-maintain-an-interest-in-life/

12.　　Parenting your Mind and Body:

While reading the book we have discussed the aspects of how we should act like a parent to our mind and body and make them work for fulfilment of our life and achieving our purpose or goal in life. I have tried to use several statements repeatedly and in different sections of the book with different examples, to make sure that the concept sounds familiar to you and well known by the time you finish reading this book. We have discussed how by being a parent we can create the rules for our life and set a process for all our activities so that we can be disciplined and is able to form a habit by way of repeated action in lines of our set rules. We discussed how we need not indulge in activities based on our senses of pleasure of our body and also ignore the instructions of our mind in certain situations. However, in implementing these we also need to bear in mind and pay attention to the fact that leading a life of strictest discipline and rule may put undue pressure on us and form stress and that in turn may also cause an imbalance and the dis-alignment of our spirit, soul and body. Just like a loving parent takes care of his/her child by taking care of his routine and also at times gives in to the child's wishes and fulfils his desires, we also as a parent need to be loving towards our body and mind and not only form strictures and rules but also take care of its pleasures and desires to be in complete unison and harmony. We have to take care that fulfilling wishes to take care of the pleasures that the mind and body is asking for does not harm us in the long run. Occasional Indulgence is permissible but is dependent on situations. Let me give you an example. Suppose a child asks for a chocolate, you as a parent can very well decide to buy him a chocolate. Now suppose the child asks for a knife to play with. What will you do? Similar is the case when you are parenting your mind and body. Your body seeking pleasure in chocolate cake is very different from the scenario when your body is seeking pleasure through rash driving or say uncontrolled alcohol consumption. This is where your decision making comes into play and you need to rationally be a strict yet loving parent so that you experience inner peace and equanimity.

The way to train your mind for acquiring the right parenting technique is being in a calm and composed state of mind. Observe every point of action and take a pause before you act. Weigh out the possibilities of outcome and take your decision. A structured way of decision making will help you make the right choice and act accordingly. So, let us be a loving parent and love your mind and body and create a beautiful environment within ourselves to nurture our two beloved children - Mind and Body.

Just like we have been made to write our lessons and practice them again in again in our school and college days and we saw how students who did a disciplined practice and studied at home repeatedly could score better in exams, in our real life also we need to write down our goals and action plans regularly and track them daily so as to become successful. It is said that when our fingers write down the plans and thoughts it directly goes to the subconscious part of our brain and we tend to have an alignment of our mind and body. This simple trick when used diligently actually produces positive output.

Coming to the closure of this discussion let me just give you a gentle reminder. Many of the points discussed are not coming to you for the first time and I am sure you were knowing and have experienced in your life, but maybe were not consciously aware of or fall short of will power to come out of fear of unknown or comfort zone. Who doesn't know the benefits of Healthy eating? Why then does it become so difficult to practice healthy eating? Believe me many of you are completely knowledgeable about many of the actions recommended, but as is said, knowing is not enough unless put into practice. All this information and knowledge goes to vain and is useless, unless you cautiously and consciously practice them again and again till it becomes a part of your subconscious mind and gets automated in your system. Plan all your GYM sessions and activities in such a way that you do not need the support of your will power. Save the energy of will power to face and overcome new challenges. Keep a journal to record your GOALs, plan of action & track your progress daily till your Habit is formed and you have achieved your desired Goal.

Once you have mastered the ART OF LIVING IN HARMONIUS ALIGNMENT, you become HAPPY and SUCCESSFUL.

****

"The fact that I can plant a seed and it becomes a flower, share a bit of knowledge and it becomes another's, smile at someone and receive a smile in return, are to

me *continual* *spiritual* *exercises.*"- Leo Buscaglia[42]

****

---

[42] https://www.goodreads.com/quotes/232848-the-fact-that-i-can-plant-a-seed-and-it

13.   References

1. "A Good Laugh and a Long Sleep Are the Best Cures in the Doctor's Book. – Irish Proverb – Philosophy Through Photography." *Philosophy Through Photography*, https://philosophyvia.photos/2019/02/23/a-good-laugh-and-a-long-sleep-are-the-best-cures-in-the-doctors-book-irish-proverb/.

2. "Benjamin Franklin - Early to Bed and Early to Rise Makes a..." *BrainyQuote*, https://www.brainyquote.com/quotes/benjamin_franklin_564198. Accessed 5 Jan. 2021.

3. Bloem, Craig. "Why Successful People Wear the Same Thing Every Day | Inc.Com." *Inc.Com*, Inc., 20 Feb. 2018, https://www.inc.com/craig-bloem/this-1-unusual-habit-helped-make-mark-zuckerberg-steve-jobs-dr-dre-successful.html.

4. "Body, Mind and Soul Connection | Health Wellness & Sickness." *Sanjeevini Spiritual Healing Center*, http://sshc.in/?p=1584. Accessed 5 Jan. 2021.

5. "Body Quotes & Sayings (Our Bodies, Anatomy, Blood, Health, Wellness, Body Awareness, Nudity, Etc)." *The Quote Garden - Quotes, Sayings, Quotations, Verses*, https://www.quotegarden.com/body.html. Accessed 5 Jan. 2021.

6. "Health Quotes | Inspiring Thru Quotes." *Inspiring Thru Quotes*, https://www.facebook.com/WordPresscom, 16 Jan. 2011, https://inspiringthruquotes.wordpress.com/health-q.

7. "Health Quotes for a Healthy Body, Mind, and Soul | — YourSelfQuotes.Com." *YourSelf Quotes*, https://www.facebook.com/yourselfquotes, 11 Nov. 2020, https://www.yourselfquotes.com/health-quotes-for-body-mind-soul/.

8. "How Yoga Changes Your Brain - Yoga Medicine." *Yoga Medicine*, 25 Apr. 2019, https://yogamedicine.com/how-yoga-changes-your-brain/.

9. "Jeanette Jenkins - Greatest Physiques." *Greatest Physiques*, https://www.greatestphysiques.com/female-physiques/jeanette-jenkins/. Accessed 5 Jan. 2021.

10. "'Physical Fitness Is Not Only One of the Most Important Keys to a Healthy Body, It Is the Basis of Dynamic and Creative Intellectual Activity.' - John F. Kenned... | Physical Fitness, Healthy Body, Motivational Images." *Pinterest*, https://in.pinterest.com/pin/314477986451349175/. Accessed 5 Jan. 2021.

11. "Physical Fitness Is Not Only One of the Most Important Keys to a Healthy Body, It Is the Basis of Dynamic and Creative Intellectual Activity. by John F. Kennedy · MindZip." *MindZip - Remember Everything You Learn!*,

https://mindzip.net/fl/@edy1/quotes/physical-fitness-is-not-only-one-of-the-most-important-keys-to-a-healthy-body-it-is-the-basis-of-dynamic-and-creative-intellectual-activity-331929bf-7a1c-498d-815c-9514b976f2bc. Accessed 5 Jan. 2021.

12. "Quote by Adelle Davis: 'Eat Breakfast like a King, Lunch like a Prince,...'" *Goodreads | Meet Your next Favorite Book*, https://www.goodreads.com/quotes/87390-eat-breakfast-like-a-king-lunch-like-a-prince-and.

13. "Quote by Buddha: 'We Are What We Think. All That We Are Arises Wi...'" *Goodreads | Meet Your next Favorite Book*, https://www.goodreads.com/quotes/1349139-we-are-what-we-think-all-that-we-are-arises

14. "Quote by Jeremy Aldana: 'A Man's Spirit Is Free, but His Pride Binds Him...'" *Goodreads | Meet Your next Favorite Book*, https://www.goodreads.com/quotes/380805-a-man-s-spirit-is-free-but-his-pride-binds-him.

15. "Soul Mind and Body." *The Trivedi Effect*, 1 Nov. 2013, https://www.trivedieffect.com/inspiration-blog/soul-mind-and-body/.

16. "Spirit Mind Body Health – A Christian Perspective on God's Design of Man." *Faith and Health Connection — A Christian Perspective on Health and Wellness.*, https://www.faithandhealthconnection.org/the_connection/spirit-soul-and-body/. Accessed 5 Jan. 2021.

17. "The Intuitive Mind Is a Sacred Gift and the Rational Mind Is a Faithful Servant – Quote Investigator." *Quote Investigator – Tracing Quotations*, https://quoteinvestigator.com/2013/09/18/intuitive-mind/. Accessed 5 Jan. 2021.

18. "The Psychology of Willpower: Training the Brain for Better Decisions." *PositivePsychology.Com*, https://www.facebook.com/positivepsychologycourses, 2 Oct. 2016,

https://positivepsychology.com/psychology-of-willpower/.

19. "The Willpower Instinct Quotes by Kelly McGonigal." *Goodreads | Meet Your next Favorite Book*, https://www.goodreads.com/work/quotes/17553514-the-willpower-instinct-how-self-control-works-why-it-matters-and-what.

20. "'Those Who Think They Have No Time for Exercise Will Sooner or Later Have to Find Time for Illness.' ~Edward Stanley #quote… | Fitness Motivation, Exercise, Fitness." *Pinterest*, https://www.pinterest.co.uk/pin/13581236360887493/.

21. Wener-Fligner, Zach. "Why Mark Zuckerberg Wears the Same T-Shirt Every Day — Quartz." *Quartz*, Quartz, https://qz.com/292993/why-mark-zuckerberg-wears-the-same-teeshirt-every-day/.

22. "Your Emotions Are the Slaves to Your Thoughts, and You Are the Slave t… Quote by Elizabeth Gilbert, Eat Pray Love: One

Woman's Search for Everything Across Italy, India and Indonesia - QuotesLyfe." *Quoteslyfe*, https://www.quoteslyfe.com/quote/Your-emotions-are-the-slaves-to-your-1942

23. *Https://Quotecatalog.Com/Quote/Oscar-Wilde-i-Dont-Want-to-VpZDR41*

24. *Amazon.Com: Online Shopping for Electronics, Apparel, Computers, Books, DVDs & More,* https://www.amazon.com/Rajashree-Chakraborty/e/B08P53PDJ9?ref=dbs_a_mng_rwt_scns_share.

25. https://www.brainyquote.com/quotes/pierre_teilhard_de_chardi_160888

26. https://mindzip.net/fl/@edy1/quotes/health-is-like-money-we-never-have-a-true-idea-of-its-value-until-we-lose-it-57c3bf77-bb29-45d0-a4bb-17180e6840dd

27. "Every Time You Eat or Drink, You Are Either Feeding Disease or Fighting It.' - Healthy

Harford." *Healthy Harford*, 29 May 2018, https://www.healthyharford.org/beware-diet-is-a-four-letter-word-2

28. "Improving Your Business Through a Culture of Health | Harvard University." *Harvard Online Courses*, 21 Mar. 2018, https://online-learning.harvard.edu/course/improving-your-business-through-culture-health?delta=0.

29. https://www.quora.com/Why-did-Gandhiji-say-Bura-mat-dekho-bura-mat-suno-bura-mat-bolo-instead-of-acchha-dekho-acchha-bolo-acchha-suno

30. "It Is Health That Is the Real Wealth and Not Pieces of Gold and Silver. "Mahatma Gandhi | Mahatma Gandhi, Prishtina, Yoga." Pinterest, https://in.pinterest.com/pin/392446555004263055/. Accessed 9 Jan. 2021.

31. "Quote by Matshona Dhliwayo: 'To Strengthen the Body's Muscles, Exercise; The...'"

Goodreads | Meet Your next Favorite Book, https://www.goodreads.com/quotes/8614498-to-strengthen-the-body-s-muscles-exercise-the-mind-s-muscles-read.

32. https://medium.com/@dhanraj_acharya/computer-science-analogy-for-your-body-mind-and-soul-807a2f87228d

33. Health Quotes for a Healthy Body, Mind, and Soul | — YourSelfQuotes.com

34. https://www.youtube.com/watch?v=BLEYCyrLpkI&t=1368s

35. https://rentwear.com/work-uniforms-relieve-stress/

36. https://www.briantracy.com/blog/personal-success/understanding-your-subconscious-mind/

37. https://www.youtube.com/watch?v=QX_0y9614HQ

38. "The Willpower Instinct Quotes by Kelly McGonigal." Goodreads | Meet Your next Favorite Book, https://www.goodreads.com/work/quotes/17553514-the-willpower-instinct-how-self-

control-works-why-it-matters-and-what.

39. "Quote by Adolf Hitler: 'If Freedom Is Short of Weapons, We Must Compens...'" Goodreads | Meet Your next Favorite Book, https://www.goodreads.com/quotes/218561-if-freedom-is-short-of-weapons-we-must-compensate-with. Accessed 10 Jan. 2021.

40. https://www.goodreads.com/quotes/431935-but-feelings-can-t-be-ignored-no-matter-how-unjust-or

41. https://goop.com/wellness/spirituality/trust-the-gut-harnessing-intuition/

42. https://quoteinvestigator.com/2013/09/18/intuitive-mind/

43. https://www.faithandhealthconnection.org/the_connection/spirit-soul-and-body/

44. https://themindfool.com/pave-your-way-to-god-through-mind-body-soul-and-spirit/

45. http://sshc.in/?p=1584

46. To Ensure Good Health: Eat Lightly, Breathe Deeply, Live Moderately, Cultivate Cheerfulness, and Maintain an Interest in Life. - Tiny Buddha." Tiny Buddha, https://www.facebook.com/tinybuddha, https://tinybuddha.com/wisdom-quotes/to-ensure-good-health-eat-lightly-breathe-deeply-live-moderately-cultivate-cheerfulness-and-maintain-an-interest-in-life/.

47. https://www.goodreads.com/quotes/232848-the-fact-that-i-can-plant-a-seed-and-it

48. https://www.goodreads.com/quotes/1349139-we-are-what-we-think-all-that-we-are-arises

49. https://www.kenshowellness.com/blog/2018/10/20/what-is-the-body-mind-spirit-connection

50. https://goop.com/wellness/spirituality/the-four-bodies/

51. https://www.bridgeshealingcenters.com/what-does-mind-body-and-spirit-truly-mean/

****

****

14.   Acknowledgment

I want to extend my sincere thanks and heartfelt gratitude to some of my mentors who have inspired, guided, and motivated me to gain knowledge. Their inspiration and guidance urged me to practice the Art of Being Happy and Equanimous. Their motivational support encouraged me to think about how I can make my contribution to the society by writing out my learnings and experiences and make peoples path of life easy, happy and successful.

1. My father, the late Abanish Banerjee, inspired me through his disciplined lifestyle and Yoga and meditation practice. He was always very calm, composed, healthy, and happy till the time he lived. Even at 88, he was in an ideal health condition with perfect heart functioning, normal blood sugar level, and no ailments. I am highly inspired and motivated by him. From him, I developed this idea of spreading

awareness on health and mind consciousness and how to train our minds to be happy. No words can be enough to express my gratitude to him.

2. Author Som Bathla, my mentor in the authorpreneur journey who inspired me to write. During this entire process, he guided me and explained every step of how to complete my book and publish it. I must admit that without his guidance, I would probably not be able to come up with this book so fast and reach you.

3. Suresh G Bharwani, CMD, Jetking Infotrain Ltd. is a visionary who has inspired at least a few lacs individuals from different segments of society. His focus and consciousness on quality of service in education have created a benchmark in the hardware networking education domain in India and Vietnam. Jetking not only is a pioneer in this domain but maintained its position as a Leading digital skill institute in India for all

these years since 1990. An organization that continued to provide a 100% job guarantee to its students in the present era signifies his holistic ideology. He is an avid reader and his knowledge in various domains keeps educating people around him. Popularly called SGB, he has been the true King of his empire but his empathy and down-to-earth mentality gives him a position that is higher than the King. He is spiritually rich & his equanimous personality positively influences me. I consider myself blessed and fortunate to be under his guidance.

This book involves background research conducted in several countries, which is beyond my scope and expertise, so the number of people I am indebted to is incredibly large. I could never have completed this book without their contribution to this field. I am thankful to all the accomplished individuals whose insights from huge research work, lectures, training, articles, and motivational stories have contributed to my book's knowledge and added value. I would especially like to mention a few who have been great Influencers in my Life, like BK Shivani, Sadh guru, Earl Nightingale, Swami Rama and every individual who has helped me level up my knowledge.

I am also thankful to all the young career aspirants who have participated in research surveys, practiced the gym sessions, and allowed me to conclude my research projects. Their support and how they benefitted from the Gym activities motivated me to spread this consciousness to the world.

Lastly, I am thankful to you, my valued reader, for having faith in me and investing your valuable time reading this book. I promise you that with disciplined practice, you will start getting the balance and alignment between your body, mind, spirit and feel much more at ease and happy.

Stay Happy, Stay Blessed, Stay Aligned.
Experience a Harmonious Inner Circle Relationship.
Thank You.

****

About the Author:

Rajashree Chakraborty[43]

Education: **BSc Chemistry, BTech, MTech Chemical Engineer;**
Profession: **Area Sales Manager; Image Consultant; Career Design Consultant;**
Founder: **Happy Lifey; Re-Creation;**
Life Coach: **Happiness**
Authorpreneur: **Author of Self-Help Books on Happiness, Lifestyle, Health & Fitness, Meditation, Pranayama & Yoga etc.**

Apart from having an excellent academic background, she has been in the beauty and fashion industry as a model for several years and has won beauty pageants during her modeling days. Brought up in a film director & producer family, she has been quite interested in acting and acted in films

---

[43] https://www.amazon.com/Rajashree-Chakraborty/e/B08P53PDJ9?ref=dbs_a_mng_rwt_scns_share

as a leading actress. Later after marriage, she chose to go for a 9 to 5 job. During 20 years of her corporate experience and consultation journey, she has worked as a Trainer, as an HR, and currently working with a very reputed IT education institute as an Area Sales Manager.

 She is gifted with a very rare both side active brain functioning capability, being highly analytical as well as being extremely creative. She is a great leader who lives by example, a great motivator, a highly influencing Coach who practices before she preaches. She possesses great problem-solving skills and is a keen learner. She believes that being disciplined is a prerequisite for achieving any goal in life, be it Happiness, or Success, or anything that one is looking for. She likes to follow a minimalistic lifestyle. In a word, she is "Happy."

In these 20 years, she has guided more than 10000 aspiring youths to learn a skill and shape up their career successfully. Over the years, she continued her physical & mental fitness regime rigorously and is an active Yoga & Pranayam practitioner and a marathon runner. She has 13000 plus hours of meditation experience. She is a Certified Life Coach for Happiness.

 Apart from her Job, she devotes much of her time to Image consulting, training on how to be Happy, and how Happiness increases your Success in school, college, workplace, and relationships.

****

Happiness GYM was first book published in the GYM series.

Introduction of Happiness GYM:

Happiness GYM introduces you to 8 GYM activities or simple habits which will increase your Happiness. This book is a prescription to all of you out there looking for Happiness and

Success. There are so many books available today which provide you a whole lot of information on this topic. But what we see is that you gain adequate knowledge from reading the books, but most of the time, they are complicated and challenging to implement. Knowledge without action brings no result and takes us nowhere. So, we still keep our search for Happiness on and move on to the next book. The 8 Habits mentioned in Happiness GYM are simple, effective, and used for over 20 years. Even a 2-year-old can easily follow the recommended actionable. This book gives you techniques of what you should do, guides you on how you should do them, and how you can overcome any obstacles in your way in putting your knowledge into practice. It enables you to develop strategies on how you can form your new Happiness boosting habits.

This book includes many research work-based information worldwide, which sets the base for you to understand the concepts better &

make your reading more insightful. It also has many stories that make your reading journey more exciting, and you can relate to the concepts better.

This motivational self-help book will transform you and help you develop strategies to become happier. It will enlighten us on why and how we make the wrong choices and run after the wrong things hence delaying our Happiness. Once we realize how we are postponing our Happiness and giving ourselves a postdated happiness cheque, we will be mentally ready to rewire our habits and start operating the current account of Happiness.

After reading this book-
1.You learn how eight simple daily rituals can boost your Happiness.
2. Your stress, anxiety goes down.
3. You get to know your signature strengths and use them better.
4. You learn how to derive Happiness from your work and, as a result, get recognition, appreciation, and even promotion in your workplace.

5. Your relationship with others improves.

6. You learn to control your mind and develop better focus.

7. You become a healthier version of yourself.

8. You start changing your mindsets and look at things from a different perspective.

I am confident that this book will make a difference in your life because I have experienced immense benefit after using these techniques. I have also witnessed these 8 sets of GYM activities bringing fantastic results when implemented by others from different age groups and different walks of life. So, you can entirely rely on these tested tools of Happiness Generators. Train your mind to be Happy and become successful in the workplace and relationships and live happily ever after.

So, what are you waiting for? Make your life happy, peaceful, joyful, blissful, ecstatic. Enjoy God's greatest gift to You- "Your Life." Grab your copy of Happiness GYM now.

Link to purchase the e-book:
India:
https://www.amazon.in/dp/B08NZS3Z7J
US:
https://www.amazon.com/dp/B08NZS3Z7J
UK:
https://www.amazon.co.uk/dp/B08NZS3Z7J
DE:
https://www.amazon.de/dp/B08NZS3Z7J
FR:
https://www.amazon.fr/dp/B08NZS3Z7J
ES:
https://www.amazon.es/dp/B08NZS3Z7J
IT:
https://www.amazon.it/dp/B08NZS3Z7J
NL:
https://www.amazon.nl/dp/B08NZS3Z7J
JP:

https://www.amazon.co.jp/dp/B08N
ZS3Z7J
BR:
https://www.amazon.com.br/dp/B08
NZS3Z7J
CA:
https://www.amazon.ca/dp/B08NZS
3Z7J
MX:
https://www.amazon.com.mx/dp/B0
8NZS3Z7J
AU:
https://www.amazon.com.au/dp/B08
NZS3Z7J

Upcoming Next Book

Spiritual GYM